DATE DUE

Contemporary African Americans

JOHN LUCAS

BY
ALEX SIMMONS

RSVP
**RAINTREE
STECK-VAUGHN**
P U B L I S H E R S
The Steck-Vaughn Company

Austin, Texas

Published by Raintree Steck-Vaughn, an imprint of Steck-Vaughn Company.
Produced by Mega-Books, Inc.
Design and Art Direction by Michaelis/Carpelis Design Associates.
Cover photo: McDonough/F.O.S.

Library of Congress Cataloging-in-Publication Data
Simmons, Alex.
  John Lucas / Alex Simmons.
    p.   cm. — (Contemporary African Americans)
  Includes index.
  Summary: Describes the life of the professional basketball player who overcame a drug problem and other obstacles to have a successful career.
  ISBN 0-8172-3978-2 (Hardcover)
  ISBN 0-8114-9795-X (Softcover)
  1. Lucas, John (John H.) — Juvenile literature. 2. Basketball players — United States — Biography — Juvenile literature. [1. Lucas, John (John H.) 2. Basketball players. 3. Afro-Americans — Biography.] I. Title II. Series
GV884.L83S56 1996
796.323' 092 — dc20   95-16136
[B]   CIP
                                                               AC
Printed and bound in the United States.

1 2 3 4 5 6 7 8 9 LB 99 98 97 96 95

Contents

1 Man in the Mirror 5

2 Growing Up With Sports 8

3 Going for the Gold 22

4 Foul 28

5 Slam Dunk 37

6 Shoot for the Stars 42

Important Dates 46

Glossary 47

Bibliography 47

Index 48

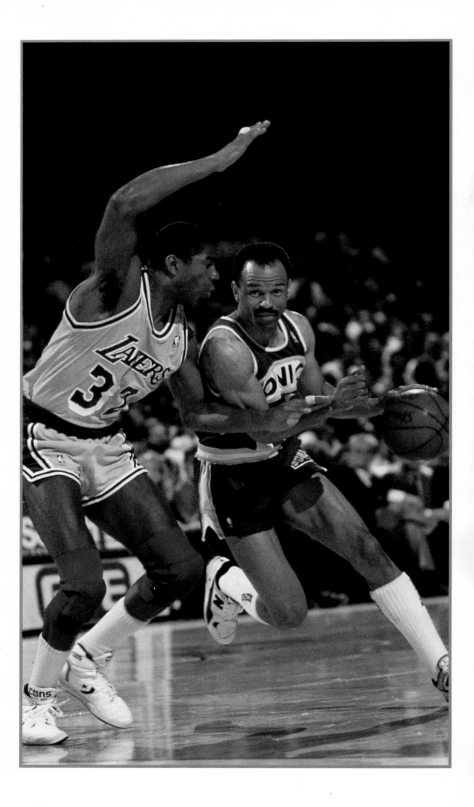

Chapter One

MAN IN THE MIRROR

"**Y**ou're doing drugs," Coach Bill Fitch said to John Lucas. "Go put your street clothes back on and sit on the bench for the game."

John Lucas sat alone in the locker room of the Houston Rockets. His career as a professional basketball player had begun with the Rockets ten years ago. He had been the first choice in the 1976 National Basketball Association draft. Since then, people had begun calling John one of the best **point guards** in the history of the NBA. Sportscasters, coaches, and fans all thought of him as one of basketball's greats. Everyone was sure John had a strong future ahead of him. But now, in March 1986, it was all coming to an end—right where it had started.

During his 1988–89 season with the Seattle Supersonics, John Lucas drives the lane against Magic Johnson of the Los Angeles Lakers.

The next day, John Lucas was kicked off the Rockets.

It looked like drug and alcohol abuse was taking another victim. People would see John Lucas as just another sports superstar who had trashed his life for the quick fix of a "nice high." Many would also think of him as yet another African-American man who could not handle success.

However, John did not do what most people expected him to do. He did not crawl into a hole to die of shame. Instead, John Lucas made a promise to himself. It was time to get clean and stay clean. He had lost almost everything that was important to him. Now he would fight to get it all back.

From that day on, John Lucas plotted his own path. First, he began drug treatment. John followed the 12-step program of Alcoholics Anonymous. He spent time learning how his **addiction** to drugs and alcohol had hurt his life. He also learned how he could turn his life around while staying **clean and sober**. Then John created programs to help other professional athletes stay off drugs. He became an important spokesperson against drug abuse.

One year later John Lucas was back in basketball. He played for three NBA teams before he retired in 1990. Then John bought, managed, and coached a minor-league basketball team. Several of the players on the team were **recovering** drug abusers and alcoholics. John's success led to another coaching job, with the San Antonio Spurs.

John Lucas, in his parents' basement in 1981, surrounded by his sports trophies. After a long struggle with drug abuse, John would once again become a winner.

John's dedication and skill on and off the court helped the Spurs become a winning team. Then John moved to coaching the Philadelphia 76ers, which was an even greater challenge. He still holds that position today. Every day brings John Lucas new achievements.

Sadly, many talented athletes have made it to the top, and then lost it all to drugs. But John Lucas is special. He didn't give up. Instead, he fought his way back to the top. Then he used his experience to help others. This is his story.

Two

GROWING UP
WITH SPORTS

The early 1950s was a time of quiet but powerful change in the United States. For the first time in many years, African Americans were beginning to push for equal rights and recognition. Individual black people were making achievements in many different fields.

In 1953 in New York City, Jackie Robinson was beginning his sixth year with the Brooklyn Dodgers. He had been the first African American to play in major league baseball. Soon, Hank Aaron, only 18 years old, would start his major league career with the Milwaukee Braves. Aaron would one day break Babe Ruth's lifetime career record for home runs.

Meanwhile, Thurgood Marshall was preparing to lead the NAACP, the National Association for the Advancement of Colored People, to a victory in the United States Supreme Court. The case this young lawyer would soon win supported African Americans' right to equal education. It was during this important

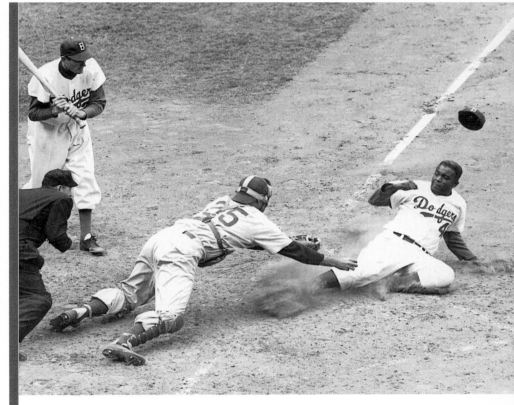

Most professional sports were once segregated. As the first African American to play major league baseball, Jackie Robinson helped win recognition for black athletes.

year for African Americans that John Lucas was born in Oxford, North Carolina.

While John was still very young, his family moved from Oxford to a quiet community in Durham, North Carolina. There, John's father, John Lucas, Sr., was the principal of Hillside High School. This was the largest black high school in the state. Blondola Lucas, John's mother, was the assistant principal at Shepard Junior

High. So John knew that education would have to be a big part of his life, too.

John's family was close and loving. John especially enjoyed time with his sister, Cheryl. They used to play a kind of indoor basketball together by racing around the house and tossing a foil ball into the nearest waste basket. Those early games may have been the beginning of John's love for sports!

John's formal education started at Spaulding Elementary School. Spaulding was only one block from the high school where Mr. Lucas was principal. Each day, when classes let out, John would hurry over to Hillside and sit in his father's office. There he would

John's family stood by him in good times and bad. He poses here with his mother, Blondola; his father, John, Sr.; and his sister, Cheryl.

do his homework, or watch his father working with his staff. John saw these visits as an opportunity to spend some time alone with his father.

John's visits to Hillside High gave him another special opportunity. It was there that he met the school basketball and tennis coach, Carl Easterling. John has often said that Easterling was one of his most important role models. Coach Easterling allowed John to watch the high school teams practice. By the time John turned ten, Easterling even allowed him to work out with the teams!

During basketball season, John would shoot hoops with the older kids. On the tennis courts, he would retrieve the tennis balls for the players. By borrowing someone's racket, John could quickly lob the balls back to the players. In this unique way, John began to develop his tennis swing.

Watching this boy in action, Coach Easterling became aware of John's athletic abilities. He began to train John in basketball, and by the summer he added tennis to the schedule.

Soon John's love of tennis grew. His father played sometimes for fun, and he had been a tennis coach when he was younger. The Lucas family also attended tennis matches together. So it was only natural that John would one day pick up a tennis racket. The big surprise came in how well he played.

John was fortunate in those early years. He had parents who exposed him to different things and helped him set high goals for himself. Now he also had a trainer who recognized his skills and his spirit. The coach did not know it, but he was on his way to helping create a future sports celebrity.

John knew he was very competitive. He wanted to be a winner in his parents' eyes. This was a main reason why John did well in his studies. Yet he felt that something was missing in his schooling. To him, it lacked the challenge he needed. Lessons were taught, facts were memorized, tests were given, and you received a grade. Then it was on to the next class.

Sports were different. Basketball was a team game. Sure, you knew your plays and how well your team members could handle passing and foul shots. Yet no two games were ever the same. Even if you knew the opposing team's playing history, anything could happen. John felt the same way about tennis. Even though it was not a team sport like basketball, every match brought a new challenge.

Competition was the key to John's heart and soul. In the summer of 1965, John started to play ping-pong at the local fire station. It was not long before he entered ping-pong championships for the region and the state. At the age of 12, he won the North Carolina state competitions. John was also fond of baseball and football. Still, basketball and tennis stayed first in his mind.

Coach Easterling spent a lot of time working with John on his timing, speed, and accuracy. John had little

High school basketball and tennis coach Carl Easterling was one of young John Lucas's most important role models.

time for social activities that were not related to sports. His closest friends were his teammates. He usually spent the hot and humid North Carolina summers at either tennis or basketball camp.

Though he saw less and less of them, John knew that his family still loved and supported him. He never had reason to doubt this. They were still a big part of why he wanted to succeed. He wanted to show them all the things he could do. John's parents had never set limits for him. They had never said that certain things were beyond his reach because he was black,

or southern, or not wealthy. As far as John was concerned, nothing was impossible.

This did not mean that John did not have to face racism. He often came across racism in the world of tennis. The game was still thought of by many as a sport for the "right" people. That often translated into wealthy white people. Many times he was excluded from certain activities in the tennis camps. In one competition, the referee repeatedly called John for **foot faults**. John knew he could never have been at fault that many times, but what could he do? At another match, John was not even allowed to use the locker rooms or the toilet!

Ten years earlier, John might have faced even greater obstacles. Now, in the early 1960s, things were changing. Wilt Chamberlain had scored a hundred points in a single NBA game. Cassius Clay, who later changed his name to Muhammad Ali, had won the heavyweight boxing title. Sidney Poitier became the first African American to win an Oscar for best actor. Martin Luther King, Jr., marched on Selma, Alabama, and on Washington, D.C.

All around John Lucas, the tides of change were rising. In his own way John was a part of that tide. He was proving racial prejudices and stereotypes to be wrong. John Lucas was crossing color lines and setting

At 14 John Lucas was competing against adults in major tennis meets.

new standards simply by doing what he did best.

Soon John began to compete in youth tennis tournaments around North Carolina. From 1964 until 1968, he played and won many competitions. The cost of tournaments and traveling was high. It might have been impossible for John to compete, except for just one thing—the African-American community in Durham. Often the Lucases' neighbors raised the funds to make John's trips possible. So when John won, it was like a victory for the whole community.

When John was 14, he decided to really test his skills. He signed up for a big tournament, the Durham City-County Tennis Championship. He entered every event that he could and won seven of them, including the men's singles. John Lucas, only 14 years old, had competed against—and beat—adults. His picture appeared in the "Faces in the Crowd" section of *Sports Illustrated*. John's star was on the rise.

During high school, John won 186 tennis matches (many against adults) and lost only 28. He was the first African American on his high school tennis team, and he won a place on the United States Junior Davis Cup Team. Some people were beginning to compare him to Arthur Ashe. Ashe was another great African-American tennis player, who tragically died of AIDS in 1993.

Tennis was not the only sport in which John was excelling. In junior high school, he was quickly promoted to the **varsity** basketball team and led the city of Durham in scoring. John averaged about 35

John was the star of the Hillside High School varsity basketball team.

points per game in his senior year and led his team to the North Carolina state tournament. By the time he graduated from high school, John Lucas was All-American in two sports.

During these years, John's parents gave him few household chores or responsibilities. They were concerned that certain tasks might damage his hands or keep him from practice. All of his time and energy was dedicated to sports. His confidence grew through sports. The admiration he received from others came through sports. John Lucas *was* sports.

Yet John's obsession with sports did not fill all of his needs. John felt out of place socially. He was used to being alone, working out with his teammates, or going out with his family. He wasn't used to parties or dates. But some people expected that a winner in sports should be the same way with friends and with girls, too.

John was a natural leader, but he was still shy inside. The athlete had grown, but the person had not. It was in high school that John tried alcohol. Alcohol had never really been in his life before. His parents did not drink. Drinking had never interested John because he was always so busy practicing or preparing for a game. Now he felt he needed something to help him relax in a crowd. After a few drinks, John felt more at ease. Whether he was with a group or going on a first date, alcohol made him feel that everything was okay.

Actually, there was only one girl John was really

John was sure he would one day marry his classmate, Debbie Fozard.

interested in. Her name was Debbie Fozard. They had met in elementary school. If he walked past her class and caught her eye, John would do something goofy to make her laugh. He was certain they would marry one day, even though Debbie did not take him very seriously.

By the time high school graduation arrived, John had a big decision to make. He had to decide which sport he would play professionally. Several colleges offered excellent sports scholarships, but he had to make a choice: basketball or tennis. Some advice from tennis star Arthur Ashe helped John make his decision. John had met Ashe several years earlier, and they had kept in touch since then. A letter from Ashe made John think about the loneliness of playing the tennis circuit. Could he stand it, or would he rather

African-American tennis great Arthur Ashe (left) was a role model for John. Here, John and Arthur Ashe share a practice match at the University of Maryland in 1975.

play with a team? John gave it a lot of thought and decided to go for basketball.

With that decision made, John accepted a basketball scholarship to the University of Maryland. There were two reasons John liked this school. First, it had an excellent coach, Lefty Driesell. Second, it was near John's family. The love and support given to him by his parents, sister, and the community of Durham were especially important now. Even though he was facing an exciting new part of his life, John did not want to be, or feel, alone.

In June 1972, John's future looked very promising. During his first 18 years of life, he had become a superior athlete in two major sports. He was the first African American to receive several honors. His family loved him. He had friends, role models, and a wonderful girl he wanted in his future. John also had a chance at a great future in sports.

On the outside, it seemed like John Lucas had it all. Yet on the inside, something was missing, and in a few years John's way of coping with his loneliness and confusion would cost him almost everything.

Three

GOING FOR THE GOLD

The late 1960s and early 1970s were wild times in America. Young people were breaking away from their parents' ideas. They wanted a new, freer way of life. Many were also calling for an end to the war in Vietnam. At the same time, women were demanding equal pay for equal work. African Americans were demanding the rights and opportunities that only white people had been getting.

In some ways, John Lucas was a participant in these times of change. His sister Cheryl constantly kept him aware of the African-American struggle for equal rights. John's own accomplishments in sports were already an inspiration to other African Americans. John Lucas had overcome many obstacles to make his way in the South. Whatever he did from now on was certain to be noticed.

In 1972, at the University of Maryland, John was learning that a great basketball team was only as good

University of Maryland point guard John Lucas tries to steal the ball, but commits a foul during a game against UCLA.

as its teamwork. Coach Driesell was impressed that John could score over forty points in a game, but he felt John needed to pass the ball more to his teammates. A lot of ball passing could make all the difference in keeping an opposing team off guard. John learned that lesson quickly.

By the end of his first year, John felt like he was in heaven. All of the university games were on television, so thousands of people saw him play. Durham was only a four-hour drive from the university, and Cheryl lived nearby in Washington, D.C., so John's family and friends could come to see his games.

The University of Maryland tennis coach, Doyle Royal, soon noticed John, too. Royle realized he had a tennis champ on campus after John beat everyone on the varsity tennis team. John joined the team and became one of its best players. He soon played the number one position in all the singles matches. Once again, John Lucas was becoming a sports superstar among his peers.

While John was getting high on sports, drugs were becoming more and more popular on the college campus. John had no interest in smoking marijuana because he knew it left most people too low on energy and drive. This did not appeal to John's competitive spirit. Yet one night during his freshman year, John tried another drug, LSD. He could not have chosen a worse night. It was the night before the first game of the season, and John was scheduled to start the game.

The experience scared John. At first he passed out, and then he spent the night curled up in fear on a friend's couch. He had no idea what kind of shape he would be in for the game. But John was lucky. He was able to score his first nine baskets.

At 6 feet 3 1/2 inches, John had the build, the speed, and the skill of a great basketball player.

Luck continued to ride with John Lucas. He had not seen much of his friend Debbie because of the distance between their two colleges. Still, Debbie did come to visit him and to see him play. Now, their relationship was starting to grow into a romance.

John was also playing great basketball and tennis. Both of his coaches thought of him as one of the most natural athletes they had ever seen. Several of his senior teammates felt John was their best player at the Atlantic Coast Conference finals. During his junior

Houston Rockets coach Tom Nissalke (left) made John the number one NBA draft choice for 1976.

year he was offered a million-dollar contract by the New Jersey Nets. John thought it over. Moses Malone had left the University of Maryland to join a pro team, so why not John?

A talk with his mother helped John sort things out. He decided to finish college. He had promised her he would get a degree in business. Later, John would be grateful for keeping that promise. With the help of his sister and one of the assistant coaches, John was able to get good grades. Cheryl was also determined that John should not forget who or what he was. She did not want her brother to be like some other African-American athletes who forgot their roots once they became successful.

So John was a good student and a star athlete. Everything was going his way. John even stayed away from drugs—until his senior year. Twice during his last year at Maryland, John used cocaine. Such risk-taking on John's part was surprising. Two of his teammates, Owen Brown and Chris Patten, had died suddenly from heart disorders during John's four years at the university. The only explanation John could think of was that both young men had smoked marijuana. John knew he wanted to live, so after experimenting with cocaine, he stayed away from drugs—for a while.

In 1976, when he graduated, John was the first pick for the NBA **draft**. The Houston Rockets offered John a five-year contract for over a million dollars. John was off to the pros, to superstardom . . . and to life in the fast lane. His eight-year addiction to cocaine was about to start.

As an athlete, he was more than prepared for this new life. Yet as a person, John Lucas had no idea what the pressures of professional basketball would do to him.

Chapter *Four*

FOUL

The coach of the Houston Rockets, Tom Nissalke, had high hopes for John Lucas. Coach Nissalke knew John had been one of the best point guards in all of college basketball.

John was a little nervous about the big change in his life. Houston, Texas, was miles away from his home and family. He felt alone and worried. Playing college basketball was one thing, but how would he do in the pros? Only time would tell.

That fall, the Houston Rockets went to work. At first, John was not a starting player. Instead he was a backup for Calvin Murphy. That meant sitting on the bench until Coach Nissalke sent him into the game. Still, it was an exciting time. John played against such greats as Julius Erving, Kareem Abdul-Jabbar, and Walt Frazier.

Part way into the season, John became a starting player. Then the Rockets signed Moses Malone. He and

John was part of a winning team during his first year with the Houston Rockets. Here, he takes flight against the Washington Bullets.

John had remained friends since their days together on the University of Maryland team. Now the Rockets were a true winning force. That year they won the division and made it all the way to the semifinals, where they lost to the Philadelphia 76ers.

Despite the loss, John was chosen for the NBA All-Rookie team. Yet, being alone with idle time was wearing on John. The Rockets practiced for ninety minutes a day, then the team members were free until the next day's practice or game.

Slowly but surely, drugs began to creep back into John's life. He was living his dream, playing pro sports, but he felt like he had run out of challenges. Sports was not enough. Life was not enough. So there had to be another way—something to fill the hole he felt inside.

John's second season with the Rockets did not go well. The team suffered a number of injuries, and lost five top players. Before John knew it, he was traded to the Golden State Warriors in Oakland, California. Whatever sense of belonging John had formed with the Rockets was now shattered. He was beginning to feel that pro basketball was more a business than a sport. Players were like pawns in a big game played by the team owners.

John headed out to California in 1978 to join the Golden State Warriors. During his first season with this team, John was still a star player and averaged about 17 points a game. Yet more and more, John found himself reaching for drugs. The fact that many of his teammates were using drugs did not make it any easier for John to resist.

During his third year at Golden State, John's childhood coach, Carl Easterling, died. It was hard for

John to accept that one of his greatest role models was gone. Soon after this, John's grandmother also died, and he found out that his mother had cancer. Change was all around him. It seemed like there was no one John could depend on forever—maybe not even himself. Once again, drugs were an easy way to numb his feelings.

One positive event during this time was that John and his childhood sweetheart, Debbie Fozard, were married. They soon had a daughter, Tarvia. However, Debbie and Tarvia lived in Durham while John

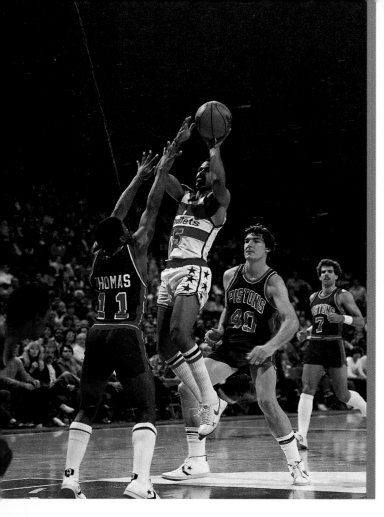

John continued to be a scoring threat after he was picked up by the Washington Bullets in 1981. Unfortunately, by this time his drug abuse was out of control.

played in California with the Warriors. He was still alone, in some ways more than ever. John began to use cocaine more often. By his second season, John was a full-blown addict. During his third season he began missing practices and games. People tried to talk to him about his drug "habit," but John ignored them. He thought he had it under control.

Soon the media were reporting on rumors about John Lucas's drug use. John hit a low point in 1981 when he missed several games. He was suspended for the rest of the season.

Desperate, John sent for Debbie and Tarvia to come live with him in California. He wanted family, structure, and a sense of belonging. To Debbie Lucas, coming to live in California was like walking into a nightmare. She had never known that John was a cocaine addict. Now Debbie stepped right into the middle of John's drug addiction.

The Cleveland Cavaliers had offered John a two-million-dollar contract, but his suspension from the Warriors ended that offer. The New Jersey Nets offered John a one-year contract. Then John got a ticket for drunk driving, and the Nets called off the deal. At the beginning of the 1981-82 season, John was picked up by the Washington Bullets. After a short time, John again began missing games.

In 1982, John gave an interview to a reporter for the *Washington Post*. He confessed to using drugs and became the first player in the NBA ever to go public about his addiction. Maybe now, with millions of fans knowing the truth, John would face the truth, too. Yet when the NBA basketball commissioner asked John about the article, John lied. He said that his drug use was all in the past. He was let off the hook and allowed to keep playing.

Under pressure from friends and teammates, John entered a treatment program for alcoholics and drug addicts. Still, he said, "I really didn't see myself as one of them. I didn't see that alcohol or other drugs were the problem. I thought I was just having a run of bad luck." A doctor sent John to a treatment center in Pennsylvania. The center treated him more like a celebrity than a person in serious need of help. So John didn't believe he had to take his problem seriously. Two days after he returned to the Bullets, he got high again.

John continued to miss practice and come late to games because of his drug use. The Bullets cut him from the team 35 games into the 1982-83 season. John called his friend, Bob Bass, the president of the San Antonio Spurs, and begged for a spot on the team. Bass came through, and John returned to Texas to play with the Spurs. He knew that Bob Bass had put himself on the line to get John on the team. Even this did not make John change. His drinking and cocaine use increased.

In October 1984, the Houston Rockets took John back. Coach Bill Fitch offered him a chance to get on track again. The only rules were, "Don't mess up, and stay clean." Yet late in 1984, after a night out, John missed a flight to a game. He arrived late and was forced to take a drug test. It came back positive. John Lucas was suspended once again.

John entered another drug treatment program, and in early 1985, he returned to the Rockets. Coach Fitch did not let him play right away. First, John had to prove himself. For months he had to sit out the games,

Houston Rockets coach Bill Fitch tried hard to steer John away from drugs when John returned to the Rockets in 1985.

studying game strategy. In the evening hours he was forced to spend time talking with the coach. Bill Fitch felt if he cut down on John's idle time, he might help keep him off drugs.

The addiction proved to be too strong. By now, John and Debbie had two children. Both children had seen their daddy come home from nights out doing drugs. Debbie found herself locking John in the house at night so that he could not reach his drug suppliers. John could see the looks of pain and concern in his family's eyes, but instead of reaching out for help, John ran away.

One night in March 1986, Debbie accidentally left the house keys in the front door. John, dressed only in

John Lucas sits on the bench through a March 1986 Houston Rockets game after testing positive for drugs. Following this low point, John would quit drugs and alcohol and begin to rebuild his life.

a suit and socks, ran out the door, locked the family inside, and went on a 12-hour cocaine binge.

When John awoke the next morning, he was somewhere in downtown Houston. His car was missing. He could not remember what he had done or where he had been. He was soaked in his own urine.

The following day John was asked to take another drug test. This test, too, came back positive. Coach Fitch told John he was off the team for good. John was out of the NBA. He had hit bottom. Now, finally, John Lucas said "enough."

Five

SLAM DUNK

In his life story, *Winning One Day at a Time*, John described his feelings after he was released from the Rockets: "I was sick and tired of living the way I was. I was in so much pain then, I didn't care if I ever played basketball again. I just wanted drugs out of my life. I wanted to be free." John checked into a drug treatment program. This time he really meant it.

John joined Alcoholics Anonymous, a group made up of recovering addicts who help each other stay sober. He began using their 12-step program to help him keep away from drugs and alcohol. This program has certain steps that addicts can follow at their own pace. It helps people learn about why they drink alcohol or take drugs, and how to stop.

Finally, John faced his addiction and admitted he was in terrible trouble. "I never let myself really feel the pain of living and losing," John would later write. Now he admitted all his feelings of pain, fear, and

John Lucas became an important spokesperson against drugs. Here, he waits with actor Robert Guillaume to speak before Congress about drug abuse.

doubt. John knew he needed to face these feelings in order to move on.

The physical effects of **withdrawal** from his addiction were terrible, too. To help himself feel as good as possible, John developed a physical fitness routine. Once again, athletics were helping John get through. He believed they could help other people, too. John began working out fitness programs for people who were recovering from addictions.

John wanted to bring his fitness program to others. He spoke to Joyce Bossett of Houston International Hospital. She agreed to let John run his program in the hospital as long as he also participated as a patient and had regular drug tests. John followed through on his commitment. This time around, he had a game of a different kind to win.

By the end of the year, several fitness programs were running in the city. Soon, John helped form another organization, called STAND (Students Taking Action Not Drugs). Then, when the Boston Celtics' number one draft pick, Lenny Bias, died of a cocaine overdose, John stepped forward as a spokesperson against drug abuse.

By the end of 1986, John was offered a position playing with the Milwaukee Bucks. He knew he would need a lot of support to stay clean while traveling. With the help of Joyce Bossett, John formed a city-to-city network of counselors and doctors. This way, he always had someone to turn to for guidance and help—and it worked!

Again, John wanted to share his success with others. He had noticed a surprising thing. There were no long-term programs for professional athletes who were recovering from drug and alcohol abuse. These athletes often needed support after getting out of a drug treatment center. So John helped set up a support network for all the players in the NBA. He also created programs designed especially for addicted athletes. These programs became part of his new company, John Lucas Enterprises. Finally, John was putting his college business degree to good use.

John played for the Milwaukee Bucks until the fall of 1988. He had a good season and averaged 18 points per game. He then spent one season with the Seattle Supersonics. In 1989, he returned to the Houston Rockets. In the world of sports, he had finally come back home. Feeling he had enjoyed a good career, John retired from playing in 1990.

Of course, John would never walk away from his love for basketball. In 1991, he bought a minor-league basketball team called the Miami Tropics. The Tropics were made up mostly of athletes recovering from drug abuse. At first, John simply intended to manage the team and to introduce them to his treatment program. Instead, he wound up coaching the team. His positive attitude and team spirit paid off. Within the first year, everyone on the team was hired to play on various teams in the NBA.

John was once again beginning to feel a sense of purpose in life. He was working hard for himself and for others. He was winning respect not just as an athlete but also as a human being.

Word of John's new role in coaching spread. In December 1992, he received a phone call. His friend Bob Bass, president of the San Antonio Spurs, offered John the job of coaching the team. John happily accepted. When the Spurs heard who their new coach would be, they were surprised. The team had never had an African-American coach.

The Spurs' surprise soon turned to joy and pride.

John Lucas coaches members of the minor-league Miami Tropics. The team gave players recovering from drug and alcohol abuse a chance to showcase their talents to the major leagues.

John's skills led them to one of the top win-loss records in the league that first season—49 wins, 33 losses. In the 1993–94 season, the Spurs won 55 games and lost only 27 games. This winning season took the Spurs all the way to the NBA playoffs.

Then, in the summer of 1994, John Lucas signed a four-year contract as coach and general manager for the Philadelphia 76ers. Slam dunk! John Lucas had managed to stay off drugs and alcohol. His family life was solid again—and now his career was soaring. John was truly a winner.

SHOOT FOR THE STARS

Throughout his struggle with addiction, John Lucas had always felt alone. The truth, however, is that he was never really without someone who cared. If John's friends and family had not believed in him, this story might have ended quite differently.

Although they were confused and hurt, John's parents stayed by him. They prayed that God would help John through it all. Throughout the years, John's sister Cheryl also tried to reach out to him and help him recover.

In spite of the nights of worry and fear for John's life, his wife Debbie and their children gave him all the love they could give. They stayed with John when the times were the hardest.

John himself has said that Bill Fitch, coach for the Houston Rockets, saved his life by firing him. Bill knew when to reach out a hand and when to let go. He realized that taking care of John would only make

Since he began his recovery, John Lucas has focused on winning "a day at a time."

things worse for John and the team. In this case, the hard choice Bill made was the right choice.

Other people, like Joyce Bossett, Bob Bass, and Red McCombs (owner of the Spurs), knew when to give a person another chance. Each one of them gave John an opportunity to change his life.

Many people close to John were there to help, but the real battle was up to John Lucas himself. "I went through so much pain to recover," John says, "because it was the one gift I had to give to myself."

Coach John Lucas guides his team, the San Antonio Spurs, during a 1993 game against the Los Angeles Lakers. John's coaching skills led the Spurs to a winning season.

Because people had helped John, he could now help others. One special example involved a talented basketball player named Lloyd Daniels. Lloyd was ruining his career with drugs, just as John had done. When they met, John tried to talk to Lloyd about his drug problem, but Lloyd was not ready to listen.

Not long after their talk, Lloyd Daniels was shot. He survived, but he went right back to drugs. A friend of Lloyd's insisted that he join John's Miami Tropics. This time Lloyd was ready to listen. He joined the team and got clean. John and Lloyd went their separate ways, but later they found themselves on the same team one more time. Lloyd was playing for the Spurs in 1992 when John came on as coach.

This is just one story of how John Lucas helped another person fight the same battle he had fought. There will probably be many more stories like it. In 1994, John wrote about his addiction and his recovery in an autobiography, *Winning a Day at a Time*. The fact that John is a person who beat terrible odds serves as an inspiration to many others. His life brings hope to drug and alcohol abusers and to anyone who has to overcome fears or hardships.

As an African American and as a human being, John Lucas faced many obstacles. In the end, he was able to overcome these obstacles. His life helped to prove that the greatest limitations do not come from the outside, but from inside ourselves. It is a lesson that we all can learn: Do not go under—go over. Shoot for the stars.

Important Dates

1953	Born in Oxford, North Carolina, on October 31.
1963	Begins studying tennis with Coach Carl Easterling.
1971	Becomes the first African American to make U.S. Junior Davis Cup Tennis Team.
1972	Graduates high school. Enters the University of Maryland on a basketball scholarship.
1976	Graduates college. Chosen by the Houston Rockets as the number one pick in the NBA draft.
1980	Traded to the Golden State Warriors.
1981	Drug problems grow. Suspended by the Warriors. Joins the Washington Bullets.
1983	Cut from the Washington Bullets. Signs with the San Antonio Spurs.
1984	Leaves the Spurs and returns to the Houston Rockets.
1986	Cut from the Rockets. Enters drug treatment and joins Alcoholics Anonymous. Founds John Lucas Enterprises.
1989	Signs on, for the third time, with the Houston Rockets.
1990	Retires from playing basketball after 14 years.
1991	Buys the Miami Tropics and begins coaching career.
1992	Hired as head coach for the San Antonio Spurs.
1994	Becomes head coach and general manager for the Philadelphia 76ers.

Glossary

addiction   Being dependent on alcohol or other drugs.

clean and sober   Not using drugs or alcohol.

draft   A system for a league of professional teams to choose new players.

foot faults   When a player steps on a line during a tennis serve. After two, the point is given to the opposing player.

point guard   The player responsible for running a basketball team's offense.

recovering   Reclaiming one's life from a drug addiction.

varsity   The main team that represents a school in competitions.

withdrawal   The process of giving up a drug to which someone is addicted.

Bibliography

Brenner, Richard J. *Basketball: A Slammin' Jammin' Guide to Super Hoops*. New York: Time, 1990

Lucas, John, with Joseph Moriarity. *Luke's Way*. Center City, MN: Hazelden, 1994.

Lucas, John, with Joseph Moriarity. *Winning a Day at a Time*. Center City, MN: Hazelden, 1994.

Abdul-Jabbar, Kareem, 28
Alcoholics Anonymous, 6, 37
Ashe, Arthur, 16, 19, 20
Atlantic Coast Conference, 26

Bass, Bob, 34, 40, 43
Bias, Len, 39
Bossett, Joyce, 38, 39, 43
Boston Celtics, 39

Chamberlain, Wilt, 15
Cleveland Cavaliers, 32

Daniels, Lloyd, 43-45
Davis Cup, U.S. Junior Team, 16
Driesell, Lefty, 21
Durham, 9, 16, 18, 31

Easterling, Carl, 11, 12, 13, 30, 37
Erving, Julius, 28

Fitch, Bill, 5, 34-35, 42
Frazier, Walt, 28

Golden State Warriors, 30, 32

Hillside High School, 9, 10-11, 17
Houston International Hospital, 38
Houston Rockets, 5, 6, 27, 28-29, 30, 34, 36,
      37, 42

John Lucas Enterprises, 39
Johnson, Magic (Earvin), 5

Los Angeles Lakers, 5, 44
Lucas, Blondola, 9, 10, 26, 31
Lucas, Cheryl, 10, 22, 24, 27
Lucas, Debbie (Fozard), 19, 25, 31, 33, 35
Lucas, John
      as developer of drug treatment programs,
      6, 38-39

coaching career of, 6-7, 38-39, 40-41
college years of, 20-27
drug and alcohol abuse, 6, 24, 27, 30-36, 42
early life of, 9-16
family life of, 10-11, 31, 35, 42
high school years of, 16-20
NBA career of, 5, 6, 37, 42-43
recovery, 6, 7, 37, 42-43
Lucas, John, Sr. (father of John), 9, 10, 31
Lucas, Tarvia, 31, 33

Malone, Moses, 26, 28
McCombs, Red, 43
Miami Tropics, 40, 41, 44
Milwaukee Bucks, 39, 40
Murphy, Calvin, 28

National Basketball Association (NBA), 5, 6,
      26, 27, 33, 36, 39, 41
New Jersey/New York Nets, 26, 33
Nissalke, Tom, 26, 28

Oakland, 30
Oxford (North Carolina), 9, 47

Philadelphia 76ers, 7, 29, 41

Royal, Doyle, 24

San Antonio Spurs, 6, 34, 40, 44, 45
Seattle Supersonics, 5, 40
Shepard Junior High School, 9-10
Spaulding Elementary School, 10
Sports Illustrated, 16
Students Taking Action Not Drugs (STAND),
      39

University of California at Los Angeles
      (UCLA), 23
University of Maryland, 20-21, 22, 24, 26-27,
      29, 47